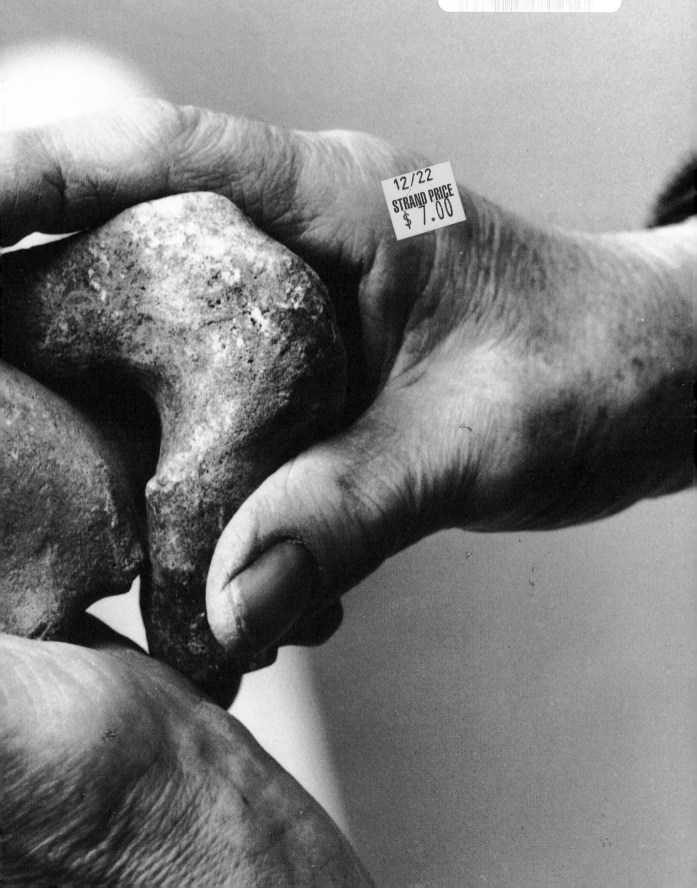

Cover image:
Composition, 1933
Walnut wood
35.56 x 23 x 15 cm (14 x 9 in)
(Reference: LH1/132)

First published in 2015 by Osborne Samuel Ltd

www.osbornesamuel.com

ISBN: 978-0-9930786-2-0

Catalogue design and production:
Footprint Innovations Ltd - printed in the UK

HENRY MOORE

22 MAY - 27 JUNE 2015

OSBORNE SAMUEL

MODERN AND CONTEMPORARY ART

23a Bruton Street, London W1J 6QG
Tel: 020 7493 7939 info@osbornesamuel.com
www.osbornesamuel.com

Introduction
By Peter Osborne

My art world career more or less began over 30 years ago when I visited the Henry Moore Foundation for the first time and met the artist, introduced by the then curator David Mitchinson, whose enthusiasm and knowledge transformed subsequent visits to Perry Green over many decades. Since then the work of Henry Moore has been at the heart of my dealing career, together with a particular interest in British sculptors such as Chadwick, Armitage, Butler, all of whom came to prominence in the 1950s when British sculpture was very much in the international spotlight.

We have had several Henry Moore exhibitions at the gallery but perhaps none quite so ambitious as this. Our last show was a memorable exhibition at Frieze Masters in London four years ago, and we now follow that with a show of rare and important small works, including some very significant new discoveries.

Frieze Masters, 2011

We are fortunate to have been offered a collection of early works that have come down through the family of Moore's sister Betty Howarth. These include a wonderful 1926 cast concrete head of Betty's son Peter and several important drawings, including two remarkable student works, amongst the earliest recorded works by the artist and clearly indicative of his precocious talent, even before he came down to London to begin his studies at the Royal College of Art. None of these works has been seen in public before.

We are also fortunate to have secured for this show some very important early carvings, none more so than the exceptional *Composition* of 1933, one of a small group of carvings in walnut, boxwood and beechwood which were central to the advance of Moore's reputation in the 1930s. This piece was included in every major

Moore museum exhibition and is perhaps the most important work by the artist that we have ever handled. We also have the 1930 ironstone head, one of only three he carved in this stone. Alongside the sculpture of the 1930s and 1940s we have a collection of drawings, some of which relate to these sculptures.

It is always a thrill to make new discoveries and we are very fortunate to have been offered an exquisite Helmet Head made of lead which we tracked down to a 1952 exhibition in Sweden. It was previously unrecorded and is being shown for the first time in over 60 years. As is a wonderful unique bronze cast from 1950 of an openwork head, again unseen for many decades.

Helmet, 1950

Maquette for Openwork Head No. 2, 1950

We have a selection of later bronzes and drawings to complete the journey through Moore's career.

Moore had a life-long fascination for printmaking and we have copies of his very first works in woodcut, lithograph and etching. The Frieze from 1921 is of particular interest, one of only two or three copies that have survived, also the earliest experimental proof for a 1949 lithograph which was never editioned. The important 1949 drawing of Three Female Figures was intended as a maquette for a lithograph that was never editioned. The catalogue is arranged so that the evolution of Moore's art can be seen. Moore's drawings are essential to understanding his sculpture and unsurprisingly are often titled, 'Studies for Sculpture'. Perhaps his best known drawings are from the Shelter Sketchbook and we have two studies from this.

Three Female Figures, 1949

Heartfelt thanks to the daughter and granddaughters of Moore's sister Elizabeth Howarth for entrusting their collection to us and to other lenders from as far away as Australia and USA.

As always we are grateful to the Henry Moore Foundation for their support and advice, to the contributors to the exhibition for their generosity and to David Mitchinson whose depth of knowledge and insight into Henry Moore is unparalleled. David met with Mary Shepherd, Moore's niece, and has kindly contributed an essay which tells the family story.

My thanks also to Tania Sutton for curating the exhibition. We are a busy gallery with an ambitious programme of exhibitions and art fairs and it is quite a challenge to pull together a show of this quality. Many of the works are for sale, so do contact us if you would like more information. And we are always interested to hear from collectors of Moore's work.

Peter Osborne
May 2015

The Howarth Collection

It is always a pleasure and often somewhat of a surprise to discover work by a well known artist which is new to the market. In the case of the eight pieces by Henry Moore that make up the core of this exhibition the fact that they remained hidden in the collection of one of the artist's sisters and her family for more than eighty years gives them a unique significance. One immediately wishes to know more about their history and the circumstances that led to their acquisition. The Howarth Collection belonged to Moore's sister Elizabeth. Born in 1894, and always known in the family as 'Auntie Betty', she was four years older than her brother. Their parents, Raymond Spencer Moore and Mary Baker married in 1885 and over the next sixteen years produced eight children: Annie, the eldest born in 1886, was followed by Raymond, Alfred, Willie, Mary, Betty, Henry and Elsie. Willie and Elsie died young. Alfred, following some youthful indiscretion went off to Canada and was never heard from again. Annie married, and surpassed her mother in the children stakes by producing nine. Raymond junior, Mary and Betty all became teachers, a profession that Raymond senior had destined for Henry as well.

Castleford, the mining town in West Yorkshire where the family lived at the end of the nineteenth century had then around 20,000 inhabitants with mining, pottery and glass bottle production providing its main employment. Raymond Spencer Moore, involved with mining in some way throughout his working life and finally becoming under-manager of Wheldale Colliery, was determined that none of his sons followed him underground and that all his children should be well educated. As he had left school at the age of nine and was largely self-taught he was highly conscious that a good education led to social dignity and mobility. Of Betty's upbringing and schooling nothing is recorded nor are the childhood relationships between Henry and his siblings. Sadly, 2015 is too late in time for personal anecdote to add anything to our understanding of their school or family life a century ago. Henry had been badly affected by the death of Elsie, his younger sister, which occurred when he was seventeen but whether as a child or teenager he had much in common with his elder sisters has not been recorded. Given the differences between them in age it would seem doubtful that they shared friends or interests.

After elementary school Henry entered Castleford Secondary School in 1910. His brother Raymond and sister Mary both attained scholarships at their first attempt; nothing is known of Betty's educational achievement. Henry botched both his first and second efforts to get into the school but with characteristic bravura partly blamed his father on the grounds that he had made him take violin lessons three nights a week. This he asserted had disrupted his studies of literature and mathematics. Abandoning the violin, he succeeded at his third attempt and remained at the school for the next five years. In his education he was fortunate, as the school's headmaster, 'Toddy' Dawes, was progressive in outlook for the standards of the day, with wide ranging interests that included art, architecture, history and the theatre. His art teacher, Alice Gostick, whose encouragement Henry acknowledged throughout his life, provided stimulation for his artistic development. Both were internationalists by instinct as well as training with experience of the world far beyond the parochialism of west Yorkshire.

By the end of his schooling Henry was keen to become a professional artist but at his father's insistence took a student teaching post at his old elementary school, replacing older members of staff who had left to fight in the First World War. Henry himself would shortly follow. After his eighteenth birthday he journeyed south to London for the first time and joined the Civil Service Rifles, remaining in the army from 1917 to 1919. Some of his letters from this period written to Alice Gostick have survived, sadly any to his family and to Betty in particular, have not. On returning home from the horrors of war there was now no question of acceding to his father's wishes for him to become a teacher. He applied for and received an ex-serviceman's grant to attend Leeds School of Art which he entered in September 1919, commuting each day by train from Castleford.

Throughout the period of Henry's education and war service Betty remained at home, though 'home' changed its location around the town. Sometime in 1911 the family moved from 30 Roundhill Road, the small two-up two-down house where Henry had been born, to 56 Smawthorne Lane, a larger property in a better street. With his eldest sister Annie leaving home to get married, Alfred vanishing and his brother Raymond, already qualified to teach, contributing to the family income, more money and space became available. Henry had his own bicycle and took full advantage of it to explore the open landscape beyond the town. Included in his excursions was St Oswald's church in the village of Methley, where his parents had married. Within the church were carved alabaster grave effigies of Lionel, 6th Lord Wells – a Lancastrian baron killed at the battle of Towton in 1461 – and his wife, the first sculpture Moore recalled having seen. In May 1914, just prior to the outbreak of war, the family moved again, this time to 37 Briggs Avenue, situated on the outskirts of Castleford, right on the edge of the countryside.

The beginning of the 1920s brought many changes for the Moore family. Betty married Rowland Howarth, another teacher, in March 1921 and moved to Mulbarton, just south of Norwich. Brother Raymond now 34 had also married in 1921. He went to work near Downham Market at a school in the village of Stoke Ferry. The family's break with Yorkshire became final the following year when, for the sake of Raymond Spencer Moore's declining health, he and his wife followed their children to Norfolk. Betty's still unmarried sister Mary took a teaching post in Wighton, a pretty village just behind Wells-next-the-Sea, and moved into the School House which had plenty of room to accommodate her parents. Henry, having won a scholarship from Leeds in 1921 to the Royal College of Art had already left Castleford for digs in London. Sadly for Raymond senior, the move came too late. He died in 1922 and was buried in the graveyard at Wighton. Decades later, when staff from the Henry Moore Foundation were working on the exhibition *Henry Moore and the Sea*, being held during 1993 in Wighton's School House, which by then had become a gallery, Raymond's gravestone, a white marble cross with simple lettering, was discovered in the nearby churchyard. Now broken, arrangements were made for it to be removed to Perry Green where it was

carefully restored by Michel Muller, one of Moore's last assistants. Its later reinstatement in Wighton provided a poignant moment for friends and family alike.

Henry became a regular holiday visitor to both his sisters' homes during the 1920s, spending time with his mother while carving and drawing in the fresh Norfolk air and collecting pebbles from the beach. Some of the earliest photographs of him working out of doors were taken at this time. He also carved at Mulbarton, though here it wasn't all work, as he babysat for the Howarths after the birth of their son Peter in 1922, and their daughter Mary four years later. In the early 1930s, prompted by Rowland becoming headmaster of Waldershare School, near Dover – and where Betty taught the infant class, the Howarths moved to Tilmanstone, a village in the middle of the east Kent colliery. Their move proved a catalyst for Henry. It seems likely that they had some influence in his decision to find a country property in the same vicinity. Henry, who graduated from the Royal College of Art in 1924 stayed on to teach and in 1929 married Irina Radetsky, a painting student at the college. He purchased a studio flat in Hampstead shortly after the wedding but needing greater working space followed his sister and brother-in-law to Kent. Barfrestone, a village adjacent to Tilmanstone was their first choice. Here they purchased Jasmine Cottage, originally two labourers' homes knocked into one with about sixty foot of garden, but in 1935 when Henry thought the garden too small for outside working he and Irina moved further inland to Kingston, just to the south-east of Canterbury. The cottage they acquired, more a modern bungalow, named Burcroft, had five acres of land. It became the forerunner for what Henry was able to accomplish post-war on a much larger scale at Hoglands, his home from 1940 set in the Hertfordshire countryside at Perry Green. Here, over the next forty-six years the availability of land allowed him ample opportunity to build a number of small studios in an ever increasing parkland setting, which provided a suitable environment for placing sculpture out of doors.

Image: Henry Moore carving

The Violinist, c.1919

Couple Embracing, 1920

The eight works in the Howarth Collection, all from early in Moore's development, divide rather easily into four pairs: two early works drawn in the period between his return in 1919 from the army and his move to London in 1921, two studies of his baby nephew Peter, two life drawings from the 1920s, and two sketchbook pages from the beginning of the 1930s.

*The Violinist c.*1919 (HMF 19(1)), pen and ink, brush and ink, on off-white wove paper and *Couple Embracing* 1920 (HMF 20(1)), brush and ink, pen and ink, watercolour are both thought to be connected to Moore's time at Leeds School of Art between 1919 and 1921. In the Howarth family *The Violinist* was always considered the drawing which got Moore into college in the first place. If this story is true the work would date to the short period between him leaving the army and starting at college. The image, though vaguely in Aubrey Beardsley style is probably autobiographical, drawn with a touch of irony and a slight aside to his father who had insisted the young Moore take violin lessons. Moore persisted for some time to please his parent though he knew he had little aptitude for music and far more for art. *Couple Embracing* 1920 seems the very antithesis of a Moore drawing – colourful, flat, decorative and romantic. Probably produced as a college project or exercise it has retained a fresh jewel-like quality. Early signatures included a monogram with the initials 'HSM' enclosed within a circle, the use of the diminutive 'Hal' rather than 'Henry', and the inclusion of his middle name, 'Spencer'.

Studies of Sleeping Child: The Artist's Nephew, Peter 1922, pencil on cream light-weight paper (HMF 22a) and *Baby's Head* 1926, cast concrete (LH 35), are rather unusually for Moore, both portraits. Betty's son Peter Howarth was born in 1922, just at the time of his grandfather's death – the new baby bringing much joy amidst the family's sadness. Moore's tender pencil sketch of Peter foreshadows the studies he made after the birth of his own daughter, Mary, in 1946 and again in 1977, following the birth of Mary's eldest child, Gus. While the subject of heads, both in sculpture and drawing, feature regularly in Moore's work, identifiable portraits beyond the family do not; the major exception being four pencil, chalk and pen and ink studies from 1934 of the poet Stephen Spender. The cast concrete head, made slightly later than the drawing, shows a pugnacious looking child with the material coloured green foreseeing later work by Moore in serpentine and verde di Prato.

After starting his education at Waldershare School, Peter Howarth went on to Dover County School and then to study architecture, being awarded in 1940 first class honours in the examinations of the architects' general preliminary course at Thanet School of Art. Moore had been fortunate to survive the battle of Cambrai in 1917, an early tank encounter rendered infamous by the use of poison gas. Though seriously ill, he made a full recovery. His nephew was not so lucky. Joining the RAF as a rigger during the Second World War, Peter was posted with 216 Squadron to North Africa. Still just 20 years of age, he was aboard a Bristol Bombay transporter which took off on 7 August 1942 from Burg el Arab – the temporary headquarters of the Eighth Army and the RAF's

Peter Howarth

Desert Air Force, sited thirty-five miles west of Alexandria – on a short flight to Cairo. On board were twenty-three passengers and crew, including the newly appointed commander of the Eighth Army, Lieutenant General William Gott. Unknown to the British, German intelligence had become aware of the flight and of who was on board. Moments after lift-off the plane was attacked and damaged by six Messerschmitt 109 fighters. With both engines gone and the plane on fire, the badly injured pilot still managed to land successfully in the desert allowing him and four others a moment to scramble out, but the fighters continued to strafe the wreckage, preventing there being any more survivors. Among the dead were General Gott, the most senior British army commander lost during the entire war, and Peter Howarth. To this day, Peter's sister, Mary Shepherd, remembers the arrival of the telegram announcing his death and her parents anguish at the news.

Seated Nude c.1924 (HMF 214a), in pen and ink, charcoal and chalk on paper, and *Seated Nude* 1929 (HMF 703a), brush and wash, pen and ink on paper, are studies of a seated figure facing right. Dating Moore's life drawings is notoriously difficult

Seated Nude, 1929

Seated Nude, c.1924

as few were signed and even fewer dated at the time. Howarth family tradition has always maintained the earlier nude to be a study of Irina but if that were true the *c.*1924 date seems rather early. The study may well have been cut down from a larger composition as the placement of the head just right of centre looks a little awkward and in most of Moore's life drawings is normally positioned just to the left. On the plus side, the identification of Irina as the sitter could well be correct. *Seated Nude* 1929, also facing to the right, is drawn with far greater confidence and is typical of a number of female figures shown with a leg thrusting towards the viewer in a three-dimensional manner.

Moore made several fully clothed drawings of female family members during the latter half of the 1920s, six of his mother and four of his sister Mary in 1926, and another two of Mary the following year. Mary married a bank manager in Wells next-the-Sea in 1925 and moved to Colchester taking her mother with her. All twelve drawings date from their time in Essex. Also from this period comes one drawing of Betty. Entitled *The Artist's Sister Betty* 1929 (HMF 710b), and inscribed in pencil 'My Sister Betty', it shows a head and shoulders drawn in brush and ink, wash and watercolour from slightly above, with the sitter looking to the right. Betty wears a necklace above a collarless top and has hair bobbed in the fashion of the period.

Studies for Sculpture 1931 (HMF 898b), and *Ideas for Sculpture: Seated Figures* 1931 (HMF 898c), drawn with brush and wash, pen and ink and crayon are pages from a disbanded sketchbook or sketch pad of cream light-weight wove paper 260 x 178mm, with two holes punched close to the top, to which fourteen extant pages have been ascribed. The original number and sequence of pages is unknown as is their manner of attachment through the holes. Called the *Sizewell Sketchpad* after an inscription noting *Sunbathing Sizewell 1931* on a page depicting a semi-nude figure looking out to sea (HMF 898), nothing else on the pages suggests anything to do with Sizewell or the sea. (Sizewell, close to Aldeburgh in Suffolk, became a favourite holiday retreat for Henry and Irina, who would rent a cottage near the beach and entertain friends such as Ivon Hitchins, Blair Hughes-Stanton, and his best mates from Leeds, Raymond Coxon and his wife Edna Ginesi.) Drawing content is mainly of sculptural ideas, with many individual sketches clearly connected to three dimensional works of the period. Among the sculptures identified in the Howarth drawings two carvings of 1932 stand out: *Girl* (LH 112) in boxwood and *Mother and Child* (LH 121) in green Hornton stone, the latter originally belonging to Sir Robert and Lady Sainsbury and now in the collection of the University of East Anglia, Norwich.

Despite the fact that Moore's work is well documented there may be many early compositions still uncatalogued as his. Recognising a style untypical of mature work is never straightforward and what was given to school and college friends as well as to family members can only be guessed at. Even the question as to which pieces Henry gave directly to Betty rather than work which passed to her from her mother's estate, remains speculative. Mary, the family matriarch, moved on from Colchester during the 1930s and eventually settled in Tilmanstone, where she lived in a house on the Waldershare estate of the Earl of Guildford. In May 1944, at the age of 86, she died in a nursing home in Woking. Though they met less frequently after the Second World War and Moore's relocation to Hertfordshire, Betty, accompanied by her daughter and later her grandchildren, remained an occasional visitor to Hoglands. She owned work by other artists, including a painting by Leon Underwood which her brother must have passed on to her as it is inscribed by Underwood to Henry & Irina. In addition, Henry gave her two early carvings *Head c.*1930 (LH 76) in alabaster and the larger *Head* 1932 (LH 123) in carved concrete – both of which she sold – and a few early colour reproductions of drawings, but whether she knew

Studies for Sculpture, c.1931

Ideas for Sculpture: Seated Figures, 1931

these were not the originals is impossible to tell. Her last visit to her brother was at the beginning of August 1986, the same month he died. She lived on to witness his funeral but survived him only by a few months. The last of their generation, she died following a fall in the autumn of 1986, just short of her 92nd birthday.

David Mitchinson
London 2015

The author wishes to acknowledge the help of Betty Howarth's descendants while researching this text and offers them his sincerest thanks.

Henry Moore's wife, Irina and Betty Howarth with Mary Moore

THE HOWARTH
COLLECTION

The Violinist, c.1919
Pen and ink, brush and ink on off-white
 wove mounted on board
Monogram in pen and ink lower right
The monogram of initials enclosed in
a circle is similar to that Moore used
on pottery he produced between 1917
and 1920
21.5 x 13.6 cm (8½ x 5¼ in)
(Reference: AG 19.1 / HMF 19.1)

Provenance
Mr & Mrs Rowland Howarth
Thence by descent

Literature
Ann Garrould, ed., Henry Moore Complete
Drawings 1916-29, vol.1, London, 1996, no. AG
19.1, illustrated p. 19

Couple Embracing, 1920
Brush and ink, pen and ink, watercolour
Signed and dated in pen and ink
'H.S.Moore / 1920
29.2 x 10.9 cm (11½ x 4¼ in)
(Reference: AG 20.20 / HMF 20)

Provenance
Mr & Mrs Rowland Howarth
Thence by descent

Literature
Ann Garrould, ed., Henry Moore Complete
Drawings 1916-29, vol. 1, London, 1996, no. AG
20.20, illustrated p. 24

Seated Nude, c.1924
Pen and ink, charcoal and chalk
28.7 x 17.7 cm (11¼ x 7 in)
(Reference: AG 24.3 / HMF 214a)

Provenance
Mr & Mrs Rowland Howarth
Thence by descent

Literature
Ann Garrould, ed., Henry Moore Complete Drawings 1916-29,
vol. 1, London, 1996, no. AG 24.3, illustrated p. 85

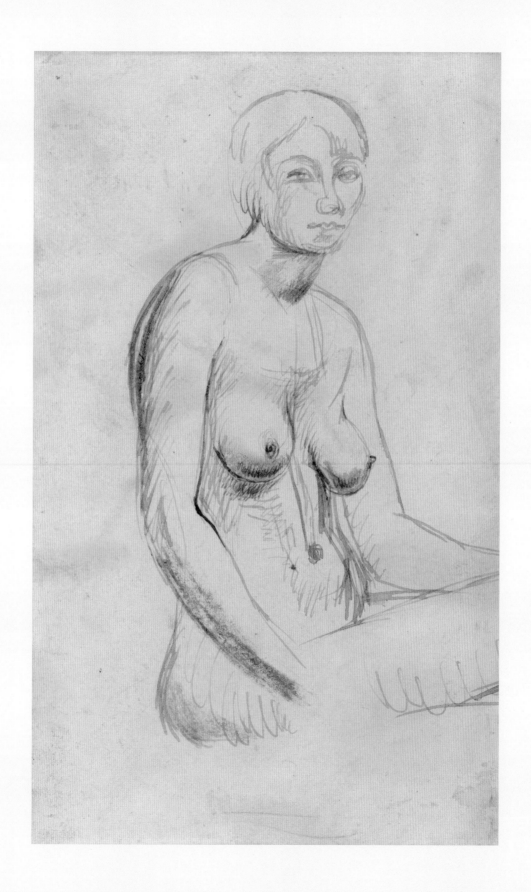

Above:
**Studies of Sleeping Child: The Artists
Nephew Peter,** 1922
Pencil on cream lightweight paper
15.4 x 21.6 cm (6 x 8½ in)
(Reference: AG 22.23 / HMF 22)

Provenance
Mr & Mrs Rowland Howarth
Thence by descent

Literature
Ann Garrould, ed., Henry Moore Complete
Drawings 1916-29, vol. 1, London, 1996, no. AG
22.23, illustrated p. 53

Right:
Baby's Head, 1926
Cast concrete
Unique
10.2 x 10.2 x 15.2 cm (4 x 4 x 6 in)
(Reference: LH1/35)

Provenance
Mr & Mrs Rowland Howarth
Thence by descent

Literature
David Sylvester (ed.) and Herbert Read, Henry
Moore. Complete Sculpture, 1921-48, vol. I,
London, 1990, no. 35, illustrated p.7

Seated Nude, 1929
Pen and ink, charcoal, chalk, wash
Signed in pen and ink lower left
42.9 x 33.8 cm (16¾ x 13¼ in)
(Reference: AG.29.18 / HMF 703a)

Provenance
Mr & Mrs Rowland Howarth
Thence by descent

Literature
Ann Garrould, ed., Henry Moore Complete
Drawings 1916-29, vol. 1, London, 1996, no. AG
29.18, illustrated p. 213

Ideas for Sculpture: Seated Figures, 1931
Pen and ink, brush and wash, crayon on cream
light-weight wove paper
25.4 x 17.8 cm (10 x 7 in)
(Reference: HMF 898c)

Provenance
Mr & Mrs Rowland Howarth
Thence by descent

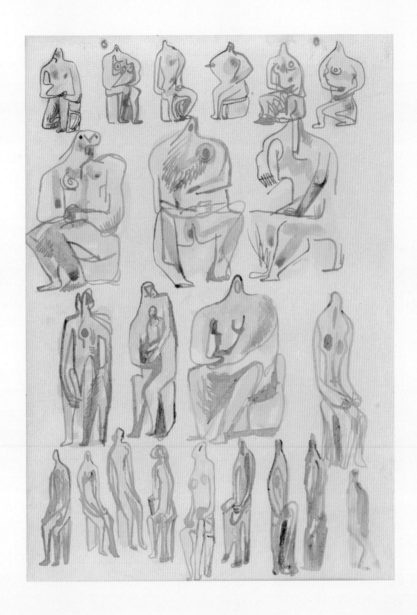

Studies for Sculpture, c.1931
Pen and ink, brush and wash, crayon on cream
light-weight wove paper
25.4 x 17.8 cm (10 x 7 in)
(Reference HMF 898b)

Provenance
Mr & Mrs Rowland Howarth
Thence by descent

Composition, 1933
Walnut wood
35.56 x 23 x 15 cm (14 x 9 in)
(Reference: LH1/132)

Provenance
Mr Douglas Glass, UK
Mr Christopher Glass, UK
Marlborough Fine Art, London
Private Collection, UK
Private Collection, USA

Exhibitions
Mayor Gallery, London, "Unit One", October 1933
Palais des Beaux Art, Brussels, 1949, "Henry Moore,
Scuptures Dessins", no. 20, reproduced.
Musée d'Art Moderne, Paris, 1949, "Henry Moore",
No. 20, reproduced.
Kunsthalle Bern, Bern, "Henry Moore", 1950,
No.20, reproduced.
Athens, Zappelon Gallery,1951, "Henry Moore,
Sculpture and Drawings"
Marlborough Fine Art, London, "Henry Moore, Stone and
Wood Carvings", June- July 1961, No 48,
reproduced.
Rijksmuseum Kröller-Müller, Otterlo, Holland,
"Henry Moore",
4th April - 7th July 1968, Number 24, reproduced.
Museum Boymans-Van Beuningen, Rotterdam,
Holland, "Henry Moore", 17th September - 4th November
1968, Number 24, reproduced.
National Museum of Modern Art, Tokyo, "Henry Moore",
1969-70, Number 10, Exhibition travelled to, Osaka, Nagoya
and Hong Kong.
Orangerie des Tuileries, Paris, 1977, "Henry Moore", num-
ber 16
Leeds City art gallery, "Henry Moore Early Carvings 1920-
1940", 27th November 1982 - 29th January 1983, number 25,
Reproduced page 64.
Metropolitan Museum Of Art, New York, Henry Moore, 60
Years Of his Art", 1983, page 32, reproduced

Literature
Paul Fierens, "Sculpteurs d'Aujourd'hui, Editions des
Chroniques
du Jour, Paris, 1933, reproduced.
Paul Nash, "Unit One", Listener, London, 5th July,
1933 reproduced.
E.M.Benson, "Seven Sculptors", American Magazine
of Art, Washington, D.C., August 1935, reproduced.
Carola Giedion-Welker, "Werk", Winterthur,
April 1955 Reproduced.
Henry Moore, "Complete Sculpture, 1921-1948", Lund
Humpries, vol 1., Ed. Alan Bowness, London 1957,
no. 132, reproduced page 81.
Herbert Read, "Henry Moore : Sculpture and Drawings,
New York, 1944, illustrated no. 77.
Franco Russoli and David Mitchinson, "Henry Moore Sculp-
ture", Arthur A. Bartley, New York & London, 1988, no. 83,
reproduced in colour page 58. First published by Ediciones
Poligrafa S.A, Barcelona 1981.
David Mitchinson,"Henry Moore Sculpture", Editions Cercle
D'Art, Paris 1984, Page 58, No. 80 illusustrated.
John Makepeace, "The Encyclopedia of Wood", Facts on
File, New York and London, 1989, reproduced.
David Mitchinson and Julian Stallabrass, Henry
Editions Poligrafa, S.A., Barcelona, 1992, reproduced
in colour, no. 26.
James Johnson Sweeney, Henry Moore, The Museum of
Modern Art, New York, 1946, p.22.

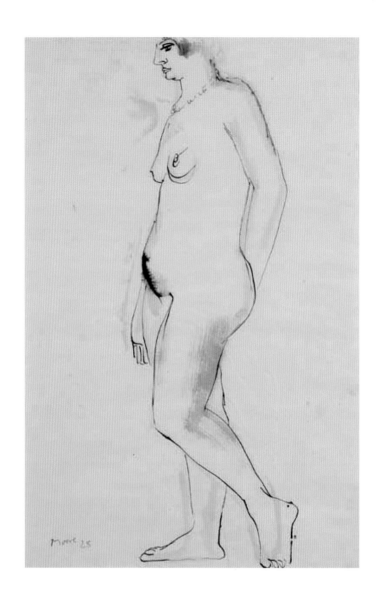

Standing Nude in Profile, 1928
Pen and ink and wash on paper
Signed and dated lower left
43 x 29 cm (17 x 11 ½ in)
(Reference: HMF 558; AG 28.70)

Literature
Ann Garrould, ed., Henry Moore Complete Drawings 1916-29, vol. 1,
London, 1996, no. AG 28.70, illustrated p. 185

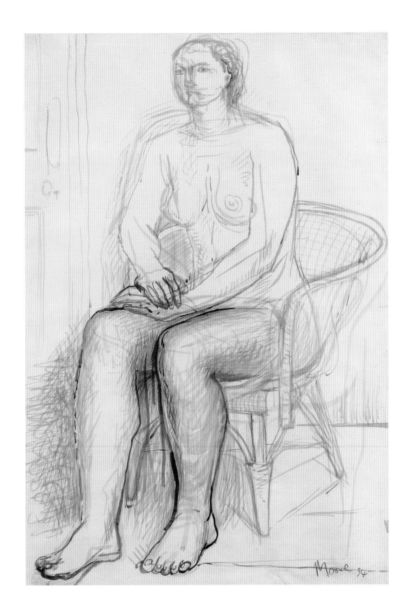

Seated Nude in a Wicker Chair, 1934
India ink, brush, wash & charcoal on paper, laid down on paper.
Signed and dated lower right
55.9 x 38 cm (22 x 15 in)
(Reference: AG34.15; HMF 1068)

Provenance
Curt Valentin Gallery, New York. Joan & Lester Avnet, Great Neck.
M. Knoedler & Co Inc., New York. Jeanne Frank, New York. Estate
of Max & Isabell Smith Herzstein, USA, Private Collection, UK

Literature
Ann Garrould, ed., Henry Moore Complete Drawings 1916-29,
vol. 2, London, 1930-1939, no. AG34.15, illustrated p. 114

Nine Figures, 1938
Watercolour, pencil & ink on paper
Signed lower left
Inscribed on the drawing: 'Think of purely
structural ideas. Spatial composition' & Spatial
composition or lead, or granite or terracotta',
together with other notes.
27.3 x 18.4 cm (10 ¾ x 7 ¼ in)

To be included in the addendum to volume 2 of
the 'Complete Drawings of Henry Moore'.

Standing Figures, 1940
Pencil, wax crayon, chalk, coloured crayon,
watercolour wash, pen and ink
Signed and dated in ink lower left
18.1 x 26.6 cm (7 x 10 ½ in)
(Reference: HMF1538; AG40.5)

Provenance
The Rita & Taft Schreiber Collection,
Califorina, USA

Exhibition
Los Angeles County Museum of Art, 'Henry
Moore in Southern California, 1973'

Literature
Ann Garrould, ed., Henry Moore Complete
Drawings 1940-49, vol. 3, London, 2001,
no. AG40.5, illustrated p. 22-23

Study for 'Morning after the Blitz', 1940-41
Pencil, wax, crayon, chalk and watercolour wash
Signed and dated, Moore'41
20 x 16 cm (7 ¾ x 6 ¼ in)
(Reference: HMF 1741a; AG 40-42.165)

Provenance
Private Collection, UK

Literature
Ann Garrould, Henry Moore Complete Drawings
1940-49, Vol 3, London 2001, no. AG 40-42.165;
HMF 1741a, illustrated p. 70

Draped Figures in a Shelter, 1941
Pencil, chalk, wax crayon, watercolour wash,
pen and ink, gouache on medium-weight wove.
Signed and dated lower right in ink
38.2 x 56.4 cm (15 x 22¼ in)
(Reference: HMF 1814a)

Provenance
The Artist
Private Collection, UK, purchased form the above

Three Seated Figures: Ideas for Sculpture, 1941
Wax crayon, coloured crayon, chalk, pastel (rubbed),
charcoal (rubbed), watercolour wash, pen and ink.
Signed and dated in pen lower right
27.7 x 37.5 cm (11 x 14 ¾ in)
(Reference: HMF1829; AG41.79)

Literature
Ann Garrould, ed., Henry Moore Complete Drawings
1940-49, vol. 3, London, 2001, no. AG41.79, illustrated p. 100.

*The depiction of and relationship between sitting and
recumbent figures lies at the heart of Moore's most popular
and recognisable graphic accomplishment, the Shelter
drawings of 1940-1942. What is less well known is that
many of Moore's drawings at this time display a remarkably
innovative and noticeably expressionist and less literal
approach to composition, both in the celebrated sketchbooks
and in the many loose sheets of that period. He employed
an astonishing variety of media in some of the works,
particularly in the present drawing where the theoretically
antipathetic use of wax crayon and watercolour is further
overlaid with chalk, pastel and charcoal. In this series of
sitting women in the Underground the artist is using the
pen and brush to move the figures around within a loose
framework, sometimes the women are occupied with
children, or knitting, or evidently chatting to each other,
often they are sitting patiently and stoically, waiting as s
o many thousands did, night after night, for the
all-clear overhead.*

Miner Drilling in Drift, 1942
Pencil, wax crayon and watercolour wash
From the Coal mine sketchbook.
30.5 x 22.2 cm (12 x 8¾ in)
(Reference: AG 42.107; HMF 2006)

Provenance
Roland, Browse and Delbanco. Mrs O de Aris,
Buenos Aires. Sothebys London 1967.
Brook Street Gallery, 1967. Christies London
1973. Private collection USA.

Literature
Ann Garrould, ed., Henry Moore Complete
Drawings 1940-49, vol. 3, London, 2001, no.
AG42.107, illustrated p. 143.

Ideas for Sculpture, 1942
Signed 'Moore.', lower right and inscribed
'Seated figure.' center left;
Inscribed 'Two reclining figures.' verso.
22.5 x 17.3 cm (8 ¾ x 6 ¾ in)
(Reference: HMF 2040; AG 42.148)

Provenance
Buchholz Gallery (Curt Valentin) New York
(by 1955). Erna Futter, New York; Estate sale,
Christie's, New York, 15 May 1986, lot 181.
Acquired at the above sale by the late owner.

Literature
Ann Garrould, ed., Henry Moore Complete
Drawings 1940-49, vol. 3, London, 2001, no.
AG42.148, illustrated p. 156.
Henry Moore Sculpture and Drawings, with
an introduction by Herbert Read, published
by Lund Humphries, first published 1944,
illustrated p. xxxii

*As its title implies this working, energetic sheet
is a graphic rehearsal or blueprint for possible
sculptures and contains both reclining, seated
and figures with internal forms, themes which
were to dominate Moore's career. Elements hark
back to the surrealist tendencies from the late
1930's but also formal sculptural resolutions
have evolved on the sheet and are familiar in
works from the 1940's onwards. The energetic
application of layers of mixed media echoes
the bony, taut surfaces of the sculptures. The
memorable drawing 'Crowd looking at a tied-up
object (1942) recalls Yves Tanguy's ocean-bed
surrealism. Ideas for Sculpture, though a set of
un-related studies rather than an independent
or cohesive narrative, contains a similarly elusive
feeling of mystery and atmospheric flux.*

PD

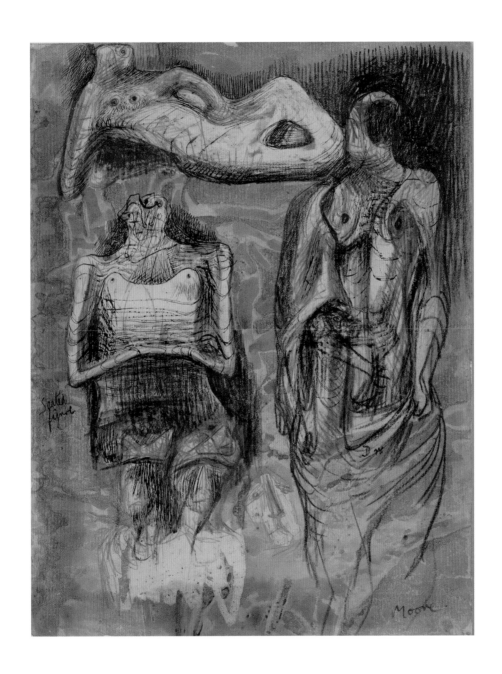

Madonna and Child, 1943
Bronze
Signed Moore, verso
Edition of 7, cast at Fiorini, London
18.4 x 8 x 7.5 cm (7¼ x 3¼ x 3 in)
(Reference: LH1/ 222)

Provenance
Acquired directly from the artist and thence by descent.

Literature
David Sylvester (ed.) and Herbert Read, Henry Moore.
Complete Sculpture, 1921-48, vol. I, London, 1990,
no.222, illustrated p.138

*In the early 1940's Moore executed a series of terracotta
studies of the Madonna and Childs as sketch models for
the Madonna and Child, 1948-9 (height 48 in) in brown
hornton stone, St Peter's Church, Claydon, Suffolk. This
maquette is the closest to the final commission.*

Madonna and Child, 1943
Bronze
Signed 'Moore' verso
Edition of 7, cast at Fiorini
14.6 x 5.5 x 6 cm (5¾ x 2¼ x 2¼ in)
(Reference: LH1/223)

Provenance
Acquired directly from the artist and thence by descent.

Literature
David Sylvester (ed.) and Herbert Read, Henry Moore.
Complete Sculpture, 1921-48, vol. I, London, 1990,
no.223, illustrated p.138

*In the early 1940's Moore executed a series of terracotta
studies of the Madonna and Childs as sketch models for
the Madonna and Child, 1948-9 (height 48 in) in brown
hornton stone, St Peter's Church, Claydon, Suffolk.*

Family Groups, 1943-44
Watercolour, pencil, wax crayon, coloured crayon
and pen and ink on paper.
Signed Moore lower right; inscribed Try this pose
over again, upper left
22.8 x 16.5 cm (9 x 6 ½ in)
(Reference: AG43-44.25; HMF 2213)

Provenance
Leicester Galleries, London. The Earl of Drogheda.
Christies, London. Marlborough Fine Art, London,
1969.

Exhibitions
Waterville, Maine, Colby College Museum of Art,
An Exhibition of Works of Art from the Collections
of the Members of the Advisory Council for the
Friends of Art at Colby, 1971, n.n.

Literature
Ann Garrould, ed., Henry Moore Complete
Drawings 1940-49, vol. 3, London, 2001, no.
AG43-44.25, illustrated p. 207.
Ann Garrould, Henry Moore Drawings, London,
1988, illustrated pl. 111.
Kenneth Clark, Henry Moore Drawings, London,
1974, illustrated pl. 227.

Odysseus in the Naiads' Cave, 1944
Pencil, wax crayon, watercolour wash, pen and ink.
Signed lower right
Pages 39 and 40 from the ` Rescue Sketchbook'
21 x 17 cm (8 ¼ x 6 ¾ in)
(Reference: HMF 2289c)

Provenance
From the collection of Lord Clark, O.M.,
and thence by descent, Private Collection, UK

Family Group, 1945
Bronze
Edition of 7, cast at Fiorini
Height: 18 cm (7 in)
(Reference: LH1/238)

Provenance
Acquired directly from the artist and thence by
descent.

Literature
David Sylvester (ed.) and Herbert Read, Henry
Moore. Complete Sculpture, 1921-48, vol. I,
London, 1990, no.238. (not illustrated)
J. Hedgecoe and H. Moore, Henry Moore, New
York, 1968, p. 176, no. 4 (another cast illustrated;
plaster version illustrated, pp. 163 and 269;
dated 1944).

A. Bowness, ed., Henry Moore, Sculptures
and Drawings 1964-73, London, 1977, vol. 4
(terracotta version illustrated, p. 10, pl. A).

B. von Erich Steingrber, "Henry Moore
Maquetten," Pantheon, 1978 (terracotta version
illustrated, p. 24, fig. 23).

R. Berthoud, The Life of Henry Moore, London,
1987, fig. 88 (terracotta version illustrated).

J. Hedgecoe, A Monumental Vision, The
Sculpture of Henry Moore, London, 1998, p. 210,
no. 239 (another cast illustrated, p. 211)

Two Seated Women & a Child, 1945
Bronze
Edition of 7
17 x 12 x 7 cm (6 ¾ x 4 ¾ x 2 ¾ in)
(Reference: LH1/241)

Provenance
Alex Reid & Lefevre, UK.
Private Collection, Canada.

Literature
David Sylvester (ed.) and Herbert Read, Henry Moore.
Complete Sculpture, 1921-48, vol. I,
London, 1990, no.241, illustrated 148.

Studies for Rocking Chairs, 1947-8
Pencil, wax crayon, watercolour wash
A page from the Rocking Chair notebook
17.8 x 25.4 cm (7 x 10 in)
(Reference: AG 47-48.8, HMF 2512)

Provenance
Robert von Hirsch
Thence by descent

Exhibited
Portsmouth Art Gallery, 1978-1980

Literature
Ann Garrould, ed., Henry Moore Complete Drawings 1940-49, vol. 3, London,
2001, no. AG43-44.25, illustrated p. 258.

**Three women winding wool
(The Three Fates),** 1948
Watercolour, wax crayon, pen and ink and
pencil on paper
Signed & dated lower left; inscribed 'The Three
Fates' verso
55.1 x 48.2 cm (21 ¾ x 19 in)
(Reference: AG48.24; HMF 2496)

Exhibited
The California Palace of the Legion of Honor,
'Six British Artists, 1950', San Francisco

Provenance
Curt Valentin, New York.
Private Collection, New York.

Literature
Ann Garrould, ed., Henry Moore Complete
Drawings 1940-49, vol. 3, London, 2001, no. AG
48.24, illustrated p. 283.

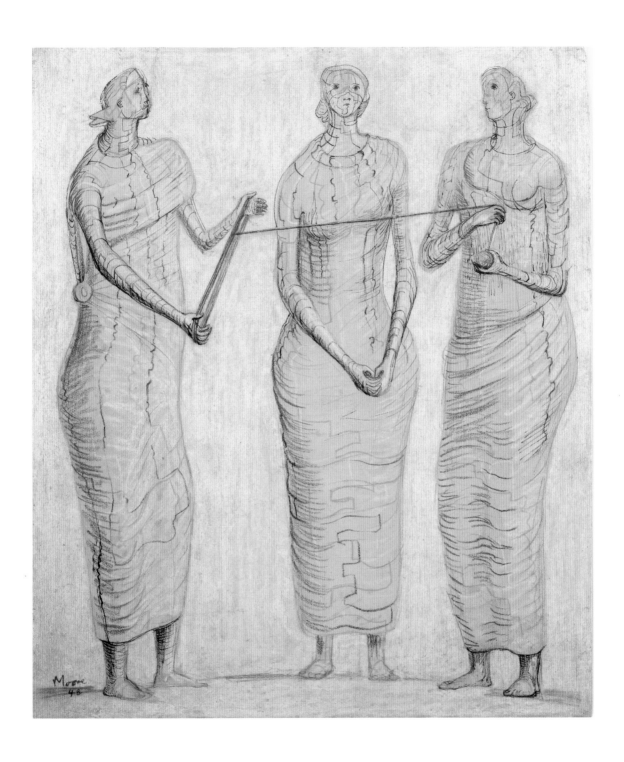

Three Female Figures, 1949
Pencil, crayon, ink & gouache on paper
Signed & dated lower right, inscribed 'Lithograph'
upper centre
29 x 23.5 cm (11½ x 9¼ in)
(Reference: HMF2436a)

Provenance
The Leicester Galleries, London, where purchased by Sir Eric
Maclagan, May 1951.
Thence by family descent.

Exhibited
The Leicester Galleries, London, New Bronzes and Drawings
by Henry Moore , 1951, cat.no.41

*Henry Moore's vast graphic output echoed the work ethic that
guided an equally prolific production of sculpture. Arguably his
greatest, and certainly most famous, drawing series was the
Italianate Shelter Drawings, documentary yet imaginatively
improvised line and wash studies based on the sleeping
families taking refuge from the wartime blitz on London
Underground platforms.*

*The war also presaged the coal miner drawings with their
Barbizon-like labour postures and dramatic subterranean
chiaroscuro. Then, with the return of peace and the birth of an
only child, Mary, in 1946, Moore continued to develop Madonna
and Child or Family Group themes, subjects that again touched
a popular nerve in the optimistic, if austere, post-war climate of
social reconstruction.*

*The animated Three Female Figures contains a cryptic,
interactive narrative while continuing the draped or blanketed
surface rhythms of the dormant shelter figures. Moore's
drawings, with their characteristic bony textures, segmented
sections and undulating lines used to describe weight, bulk and
volume, are quintessentially those of a sculptor. The dramatic
shading and highlighting further emphasises the play of light
on solid form. The drawing was chosen as the basis for one
of Moore's earliest lithographs to be published by Cowell of
Ipswich. The project was never realised and only a few trial
proofs are known to exist.*

*This mixed media drawing has the vividly modelled weight of
a painting and the trio of female figures resemble the post-war
classicism of his sculpture. A major show at the Museum of
Modern Art, New York (1946) and his winning first prize at
the Venice Biennale (1948) set him on course for spectacular
international success.*

P D

Rocking Chair No.4: Miniature, 1950
Bronze
Edition of 9
15 x 12.5 x 4 cm (6 x 5 x 1½ in)
(Reference: LH 2/277)

Provenance
Private Collection, Canada

Literature
David Sylvester (ed.) and Herbert Read, Henry
Moore. Complete Sculpture, 1949-54, vol. II,
London, 1986, no.238, illustrated p.28.

Maquette for Openwork Head No. 2, 1950
Bronze, a unique cast
14.5 x 8.5 x 5.5 cm (5 ¾ x 3 ¼ x 2 ¼ in)
(Reference: LH2/288)

Provenance
The Artist
Robert von Hirsch collection
By descent

Literature
David Sylvester (ed.) and Herbert Read, Henry Moore.
Complete Sculpture, 1949-54, vol. II, London, 1986,
no.238, illustrated p.32.

Orebro. Sweden, 1952

Helmet, 1950
Lead
Signed on the base "To Ann Zwinger from Henry Moore"
Unique
Height: 16 x 14 x 11cm (6 ¼ x 5 ½ x 4 ¼ in) (inc. base 2 cm thick)
(Reference: LH2/278a)

Provenance
Collection of the artist. Collection of Ann H. Zwinger.
By descent, Ann H. Zwinger Trust.

Moore executed a group of Helmet
Heads in lead in 1950. The present
sculpture was sold by Moore to Ann
Zwinger in 1952.

A label on the base of the sculpture
connected the work to the British
Council touring exhibition to
Scandinavia in 1952 where it
was exhibited alongside another
subsequently destroyed Helmet Head.

It is listed in the exhibition catalogue
and a photograph of the installation
has been discovered. We are very
grateful to Mimmi Brandberg for
assisting us with this information.

Maquette for Draped Reclining Figure, 1952
Bronze. Edition of 10
10.8 x 17 cm (4 ½ x 6 ¾ in)
(Reference LH2/335)

Provenance
Loula D Lasker, New York
Bezalel National Museum, Israel (bequest of the above in 1961)
Israel Museum (acquired from the above in 1965)

Literature
David Sylvester (ed.) and Herbert Read, Henry Moore. Complete Sculpture,
1949-54, vol. II, London, 1986, no.238, illustrated plate 100.

Above:

Mother and Child (Design), 1961-2
Felt-tipped pen, pen and ink on paper
Signed lower right
29.2 x 24.1 cm (11½ x 9½ x in)
(Reference: AG61-62.40; HMF 3063)

Provenance
Gérald Cramer, Geneva.
Sotheby's London, 1964.
Brook Street Gallery, London.

Literature
Ann Garrould, ed., Henry Moore Complete
Drawings 1940-49, vol. 3, London, 2001, no. AG
61-62.40, illustrated p. 163.

Right:

Mother & Child, 1953
Bronze with light brown patina.
Conceived in 1953 & cast in an edition of 7 plus
2 additional casts
50.8 cm (20 in)
(Reference: LH2/315)

Provenance
Private Collection, USA

Literature
David Sylvester (ed.) and Herbert Read, *Henry
Moore. Complete Sculpture, 1949-54*, vol. II,
London, 1986, no.315, illustrated p.39.
Alan Bowness, ed., *Henry Moore, Complete
Sculpture, 1949-1954*, vol. II, London, 1986, no.
315, illustration of another cast pl. 83
Franco Russoli & David Mitchinson, Henry
Moore Sculpture with Comments by the Artist,
Barcelona, 1988, no. 27, illustration of another
cast p. 115

Time-Life Screen No 4, 1952
Bronze
Edition of 9
18 x 33 x 2.1 cm (7 x 13 x ¾ in)
(Reference: LH2/ 342)

Provenance
Private Collection, Canada

Literature
David Sylvester (ed.) and Herbert Read, Henry
Moore. Complete Sculpture, 1949-54, vol. II,
London, 1986, no.342, illustrated p.48.

Warrior's Head, 1953
Bronze
Edition of 8
25.4 x 21x 11 cm (10 x 8 ¼ x 4 ¼ in)
(Reference: LH2/359)

Provenance
Private Collection, USA

Literature
David Sylvester (ed.) and Herbert Read, Henry Moore. Complete
Sculpture, 1949-54, vol. II, London, 1986, no.359, illustrated p.53.

Head of Girl, 1960
Bronze
Edition of 9
25.5 x 21 x 11 cm (10 x 8¼ x 4¼ in)
(Reference: LH3/468a)

Provenance
Private Collection, USA

Literature
David Sylvester (ed.) and Herbert Read, Henry Moore. Complete
Sculpture, 1955-64, vol. III, London, 1986, no.468a, illustrated p.46.

Draped Reclining Figure in a Landscape, 1973
Pencil, charcoal, grey wash, watercolour wash,
chinagraph & gouache.
Executed circa 1973/1977
Signed upper left & numbered '29' upper right
Study for CGM 473, lithograph
17.2 x 25.4 cm (6¾ x 10 in)
(Reference: HMF 3209; AG69-77.28)

Literature
Ann Garrould, ed., Henry Moore Complete Drawings
1950-76, vol. 4 , London, 2003, no. AG 69-77.28,
illustrated p. 200

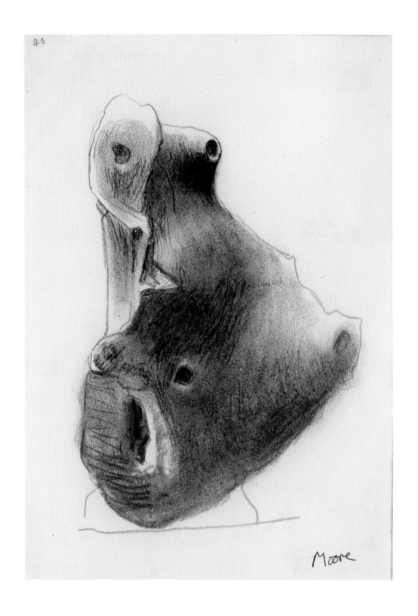

Study for Dante Stone III, 1974-6
Pencil and charcoal
Signed in biro. From Sketchbook 2, Page 37
25.5 x 17.5 cm (10 x 7 in)
(Reference: HMF74/76 (37); AG73-79.37)

Literature
Ann Garrould, ed., Henry Moore Complete Drawings 1950-76,
vol. 4 , London, 2003, no. AG 63-79.37, illustrated p. 301.

Girl Doing Homework, 1969
Pen and Ink
Signed in biro lower left
25.1 x 17.3 cm (9 ¾ x 6 ¾ in)
(Reference: HMF3227; AG69-77.58)

Literature
Ann Garrould, ed., Henry Moore Complete Drawings 1950-76,
vol.4, London, 2003, no. AG 69-77.58, illustrated p. 207

Helmet Head No 7, 1975
Bronze. Edition of 3
11 x 14.4 x 12.5 cm (4 ¼ x 5 ¾ x 5 in)
Reference: LH5/652

Provenance
Gifted by the Henry Moore Foundation to the Federated Union of
Black Artists (FUBA) collection, Johannesburg, South Africa, 1981.
Deaccessioned 1999
Private collection, Australia

Exhibited
The FUBA Collection, South African National Gallery, Cape Town,
18 February - 17 April 1983.

Literature
David Sylvester (ed.) and Herbert Read, Henry Moore.
Complete Sculpture, 1974-80, vol. V, London, 1983,
no.652, illustrated p.20.

Maquette for Reclining Figure Hand, 1976
From the edition of 9
11 x 18.5 x 9.5 cm (4 ¼ x 7 ¼ x 3 ¾ in)
(Reference: LH5/707)

Provenance
Galerie Westendorf, Hamburg
Private Collection, UK

Literature
Henry Moore: Volume 5 Complete Sculpture 1974 - 80,
Alan Bowness, (London : Lund Humphries, 1983) 707 ill. p31

Seated Mother and Baby, 1978
Bronze
Edition of 9
21.6 x 11.4 x 15.2 cm (8 ½ x 4 ½ x 6 in)
(Reference: LH5/749)

Provenance
James Kirkman Ltd, London,
Private Collection, USA

Literature
David Sylvester (ed.) and Herbert Read, Henry Moore.
Complete Sculpture, 1974-80, vol. V, London, 1983,
no.749, illustrated p.40.

Three Heads, 1979
Crayon, watercolour and
gouache and pen on paper
Signed and dated lower right
23 x 16.5 cm (9 x 6½ in)
(Reference: HMF 79 (4); AG79.4)

Provenance
Wildenstein & Co., New York (acquired directly from the artist).
Private collection, USA.
Private Collection, UK.

Literature
Ann Garrould, ed., Henry Moore Complete Drawings 1977-81,
vol. 5, London, 1994, no. AG 79.4, illustrated p. 43.

Maquette for Draped Reclining Mother & Baby, 1981
Bronze
Edition of 9
11.5 x 20.8 x 10 cm (4½ x 8¼ x 4 in)
(Reference: LH6/820)

Provenance
Weintraub Gallery, New York
Private Collection, USA
Private Collection, UK

Literature
David Sylvester (ed.) and Herbert Read, Henry Moore. Complete
Sculpture, 1980-86, vol. VI, London, 1988, no.412, illustrated p.43.

*Anatomical accuracy had long been sacrificed on the high altar of
Moore's modernistic assimilation of neoprimitivism.*

*The sculptor's reaction against the academic was aided by the
presence of drapery on the figure, a device that from the Italianate
stylisation of the Shelter Drawing series (1940s) onwards cloaked
excessive bodily detail. The reclining pose, too, contributed to a
sublimation of figurative fidelity in which the recumbent human
form took on the guise of landscape. Alan Bowness has described
this 1981 piece as one where "the mother's body is extended like
a range of hills, into the hollows of which the child can shelter.
The baby is treated with great delicacy and formal restraint, as if
Moore's tenderness prevented him abstracting further."*

*The upper profile of the figure indeed resembles the kind of
undulating moorland that Moore encountered as a child in his
native Yorkshire. As in social and industrial topography, where
human sellement nestles within sheltered valleys, the child lies
within the lowered maternal arm. Bowness again confirms how
"the notion of shelter and containment is at the heart of the mother
and child sculptures."*

*The metamorphic figure/landscape dichotomy recurring
throughout Moore's work is usually a product of the reclining, as
opposed to upright, pose. From the early reclining elm carvings
to the large reclining bronzes like the 8 foot piece in Seoul, Korea
and Phoenix, Arizona Moore could indulge in scale to promote
landscape associations within the otherwise timeless and classic
subject of the recumbent figure.*

Alan Bowness p.7. Lund Humphries 1999.

Reclining Man & Woman, 1981
Bronze, signed and numbered from
the edition of 9
10 x 24 x 11 cm (4 x 9 ½ x 4 ¼ in)
(Reference: LH6/825)

Provenance
Henry Moore Foundation, James Kirkman London Ltd, Barry O'Keefe QC
Sydney, Rex Irwin 1982

Literature
David Sylvester (ed.) and Herbert Read, Henry Moore.
Complete Sculpture, 1980-86, vol. VI, London, 1988, no.825, illustrated p.44.

Maquette for Mother and Child: Hood, 1982
Bronze. Edition of 9
Dimensions to follow
15 x 8.5 x 8.5 cm (6 x 3 ¼ x 3 ¼ in)
(Reference LH6/849)

Provenance
Private Collection, Australia

Literature
David Sylvester (ed.) and Herbert Read, Henry Moore.
Complete Sculpture, 1980-86, vol. VI, London, 1988, no.849, illustrated p.49.

Seated and Standing Figures, 1983
Bronze. Edition of 9
17.5 x 18 cms (7 x 9 in)
LH6/895

Literature
David Sylvester (ed.) and Herbert Read, Henry Moore.
Complete Sculpture, 1980-86, vol. VI, London, 1988, no.895, illustrated p.58.

Prints

Frieze of Dancing Figures, 1921
Linocut, circa 1921, on buff paper,
signed in black ink
One of only 3 recorded impressions.
16.5 x 34.5 cm (6½ x 13½ in)

*Dancing Figures is a rare and early linocut
from 1921, which came to light among other
previously unseen works in the exhibition
Henry Moore and The Challenge of Architecture, organised by the Henry Moore
Foundation in 2005.*

*This linocut was created as an idea for an
architectural frieze and conveys a sense of
movement and dynamism among the stylized
figures, giving a clear insight into Moore's
creative process at a time when he started his
earliest explorations of architectural concepts.*

*Literature: Henry Moore and the Challenge of
Architecture, published by the Henry Moore
Foundation, 2005 catalogue no.3, p.6.*

Reclining Figure, 1931
Woodcut on Japan teinte paper.
Signed & numbered in pencil from
the edition of 50
Plus 10 artist's proofs & 4 dedicated proofs.
Published & printed by Gerald Cramer, Geneva
& Fequet & Baudier, Paris, 1966
10 x 16.5 cm (4 x 6 ½ in)
(Reference: CGM 2)

Literature
Gérald Cramer (ed.) Alistair Grant & David
Mitchinson, Henry Moore. The Graphic Work,
1931-72, vol. I, London, 1973, no.2, illustrated.

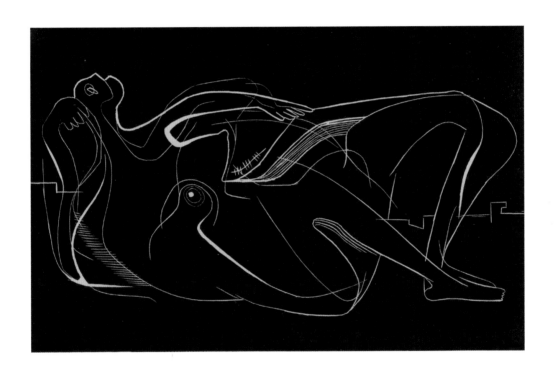

Seated Figures, 1949
Lithograph.
Proof for unpublished edition.
Commissioned by School prints Ltd London
but never edited. A few trial proofs on English
cartridge printed by W S Cowell Ltd Ipswich.
45.5 x 27 cm (18 x 10 ½ in)
(Reference: CGM 8)

Literature
Gérald Cramer (ed.) Alistair Grant & David
Mitchinson, Henry Moore. The Graphic Work,
1931-72, vol. I, London, 1973, no.8, illustrated.

*This exceptionally rare trial proof was Moore's
earliest experiment in lithography. When he
agreed to make a print for Brenda Rawnsley's
'School Print' project, the printers sent the artist
two plates to draw on. A very small number of
trial proofs of the two resulting images (CGM 6
and 8) were printed by Cowells and no edition
was made. The subjects in this print are typical
of Moore's work at the time, exploring the seated
figure, the family group and the mother and child
theme. The texts adjacent to the images (in re-
verse) are Moore's notes on the technical aspects
of this new medium*

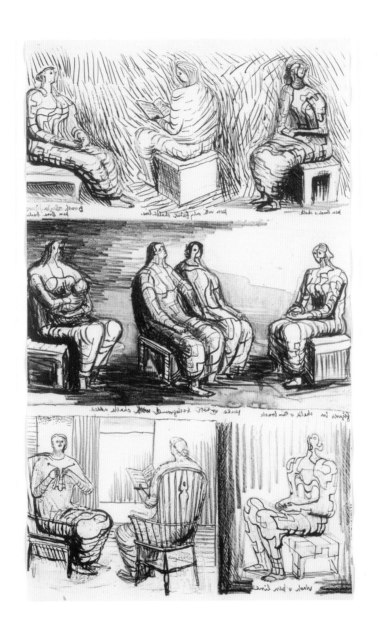

Standing Figures, 1949
Colograph. Signed, dated and numbered from the edition of 75.
Printed in three colours: yellow, blue grey and black.
Printed and published by Ganymed Ltd London, 1951.
Lithograph based on several drawings of 1948/49.
A few prints have been dated 1950.
37.8 x 47 cm (14 ¾ x 18 ½ in)
(Reference: CGM 9)

Literature
Gérald Cramer (ed.) Alistair Grant & David Mitchinson, Henry Moore.
The Graphic Work, 1931-72, vol. I, London, 1973, no.9, illustrated.

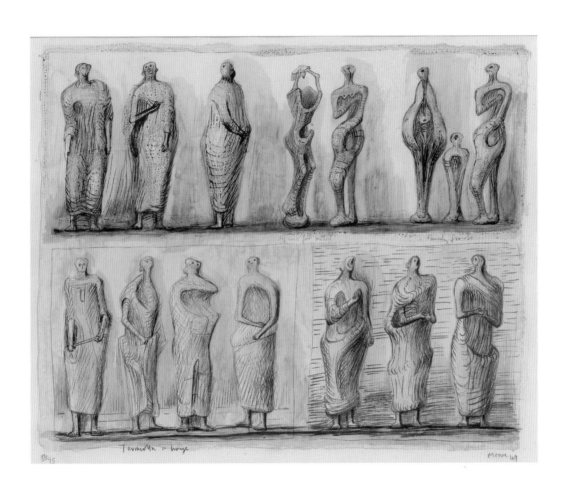

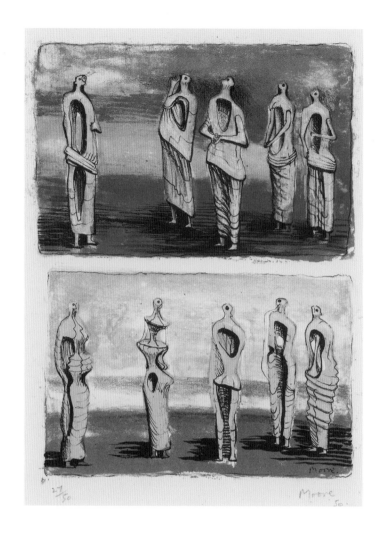

Standing Figures, 1950
Lithograph. Signed, dated & numbered in pencil from the edition of 50
Printed by W.S. Cowell Lt, Ipswich & published by School Prints Ltd, London.
Lithograph based on a drawing Standing Figures 1948.
40.8 x 29.4 cm (16 x 11½ in)
(Reference: CGM 14)

Literature
Gérald Cramer (ed.) Alistair Grant & David Mitchinson, Henry Moore.
The Graphic Work, 1931-72, vol. I, London, 1973, no.14, illustrated.